CONFRONTING THE ELEMENTS
A POETRY COLLECTION

POETRY BY SAMANTHA L. TERRELL
ART WORK BY JANE CORNWELL

MORE POETRY FROM
JANE'S STUDIO PRESS

KEEPING AFLOAT
BY SAMANTHA TERRELL

WONDERLAND IN ALICE
PLUS OTHER WAYS OF SEEING
BY PAUL BROOKES

TIGER LILY
BY SUSAN RICHARDSON

OTHERNESSES
BY PAUL BROOKES

CONFRONTING THE ELEMENTS
A POETRY COLLECTION

Text Copyright © 2023
by Samantha Terrell

Artwork Copyright © 2023
by Jane Cornwell

All rights reserved. No part of this publication may be reproduced, stored or transmitted in any form or by any means, electronic, mechanical, photocopying, recording, scanning, or otherwise without written permission of the publisher, except in the case of brief excerpts used in critical articles and reviews. It is illegal to copy this book, post it to a website, or distribute it by any means without permission.

Samantha Terrell & Jane Cornwell assert the moral right to be identified as the author and illustrator of this work.

This is a work of fiction. Names, characters, places and incidents are either the products of the author's imagination or used fictionally. Any resemblance to actual persons, living or dead, events or localities is entirely coincidental.

JC STUDIO PRESS
Design by Jane Cornwell
www.janecornwell.co.uk

ISBN: 978-1-7393231-6-5

Also available in hard cover and Ebook format.

Buachaille Etive Mòr, Glen Etive, Scotland, OS grid NN223543..

For Jennings and Sterling,

May you always seek Truth in the world around you.

All My Love, Mom

CONTENTS

Chapter I. Burning Down

10	Fix It
11	After the Fireworks
13	Autumn Winds
14	Fire
15	Experimenting With Smoke
16	Epilogue
18	Employing Light Feet
20	Circular Thinking
23	Post-Disembowelment
24	Facing Reality
25	Smoke and Mirrors
26	Escaping the Heat
27	Recollection
28	Refinement
29	Scandal
30	Dumping Ash Trays Is Messy Business
31	Fodder
32	Off and Away
33	Generosity
34	Learning to Inhale

Chapter II. Blowing Away

36	Embodying Imagery
38	Thanksgiving Leftovers
40	Ashes to Ashes
42	We Are the Wind
43	Dependencies
44	If Only All It Took Was Soap Leaves
45	Illusions
47	Scaffolding
48	Resurfacing
50	Passages
52	Woodwinds
53	Waiting for Winter
54	When the Sails Were Still Up
56	Until There's Nothing Can Be Done
57	Bleak Midwinter
58	Preparation
60	Fimbulwinter
62	What If There Were Clean Landscapes?
63	Understanding

Chapter III. Taking Root

66	Morning People
68	Alliances
70	Soul Sunrise
71	Growth
72	Entrapment
73	Ascension
74	Debunking Destiny
75	Pine Cone Prophecies
77	Latency
78	Polarity
79	Flora and Fauna
80	We Are the Badlands
83	Neolithic Era
84	Promiscuity
85	Seeking the Promised Rainbow
86	Escaping Arrogance
88	Writing My Epitaph
91	On Gravity
92	Grounded
94	Acknowledgments
96	About Samantha Terrell
98	About the artwork

Chapter I.
Burning Down

FIX IT

Water leaks from glass's cracks.
No glue.
Lend me a hammer,
Won't you?

Shattered
Shards
Seem more desirable
Than this marred,

Seeping view. No hammer
To be had,
Throw a towel
Over it instead.

The towel's stained –
Flip it over?
No, the stain
Bled through. Time for

A fire –
Toss it on;
Consumed at once,
And all is gone.

AFTER THE FIREWORKS

It's due time
To extinguish
The flames
Created by all the fireworks, from whence with
Reckless abandon
We sought
The passion
That only the lost,

And youth are wont to seek.
Then, in our naiveté,
We even tried to keep
The fire going longer, and with it, future unknowns at bay.
We forgot, amidst the temporary chaos –
Burned off fields, are the ones most ripe to flourish.

"Burned off fields, are the ones most ripe to flourish."
"The Muir Burn."

AUTUMN WINDS

Autumn-yellow mushrooms
Form belled-out pant legs at
The base of a tree,
Matching the picture I
Saw in a magazine.

You quip an age-old joke
About "fun guys" and
Old is made new again in
Our children's bright, happy laughter
Carried across the campsite, on the wind.

My face is warm, wind-burned;
Bones chilled, from its
Constant whipping
Even as the campfire laps up
Golden flames, set against dying grey embers.

The firewood and late summer season
Must both reach their ends.
But goldenrod and fungi spores are
Wind-scattered,
Ready to begin again.

FIRE

Sometimes closure comes
When and where
It is least expected,
And even unwanted.
We know time
Lacks permanence – but
Places deceive us
With their symbolic solidarity.
Through loss, the heart
Finds finality
When things taken for granted,
And things cherished,
Become equals in
The face of impermanence.

EXPERIMENTING WITH SMOKE

Smoke and fog have the
Same blinding
Effect on sight,
But not on skin.
Smoke makes tears leak
From eyes, as
Sap seeps

Desperately
From its
Heat-charred barriers, insistent
Upon escape.
No, the smoke's not the problem,
But where
It comes from –

Since even
Thick skin
Becomes thinned
When subjected
To fire.
Still, groping around
Blindly
Is preferable to getting burned.

EPILOGUE

I named our phoenix Isaiah, and
From time to time, I scan the sky for it
In this desert wilderness, where
We've learned to wash our feet with sand.

It cleans better than oil or soap,
Sloughing off – leaving only enough
Protection to allow the
Tenderness to cope

With fresh paths made
From temporary dwellings we had
Tried to make permanent, amidst
A thousand moments of distraction and decay.

There's no sign of him, and I fear the worst.
Could it be
We fixated again, on things like
Cows and birds?

Let's burn down our golden calf –
This time, leaving not even a
Phoenix to rise from
Its ash.

"This time, leaving not even a/ Phoenix to rise from/Its ash."
Peat burning, Kinross.

EMPLOYING LIGHT FEET

Let's not linger on the hot coals
Unless we wish to catch fire
From the burning embers
Continually lit by those
With rage-filled desires.

"Yea though I walk through the valley
Of the shadow of death," implies
We shall, indeed,
Pass through difficulty,
Preserving peace of mind.

"We shall, indeed, / Pass through difficulty, / Preserving peace of mind."
Coire Gabhail/ The Lost Valley, Glencoe.

CIRCULAR THINKING

I don't know if I believe
In reincarnation,
But if it is real,
I sincerely
Might have died in the Triangle Shirtwaist Company Fire,
      along with my blue collar friends,
Because it seems
We understand

A certain, fundamental,
Idea that we should look out for our fellow Man;
And that the "we," we speak of,
Is a passing of the proverbial
Buck,
Since we must, if we're honest,
Acknowledge we are the "we" who makes our own luck.

But good fortune is nearly impossible to make,
Especially when it feels
The whole of humanity
Is what's at stake,
As flames are shooting up around you. And trying to dispel
      the circular thinking of others, from inside the
      straight-jacket

Of all those obtuse angles, is little more than
A mind-game, meant to distract.

"Especially when it feels/ The whole of humanity/ Is what's at stake..."
Ineous, Grangemouth.

POST-DISEMBOWELMENT

Time-honored temple walls are closing in.
A dim beacon shines from the tower,
Warning of greed, racism, fascism.
But institutions forged
To balance and check
Are being smoked out
By persistent fire and wind;
Undoing centuries of solidity,
Replaced with repudiation
And invalidity of reputation.
Some, still-operational, automated sirens
Ring. But there are no responders,
No medics,
No one is rushing in to save
Us all from the grave
Pit we've dug
For a country gutted of its love.

FACING REALITY

Show me the way -
That way my heart knows,
But can't find
In the quagmire of
My cluttered mind.

Show me foot paths
Through damp woodland
Forests, and also
Ash-covered, fire-destroyed
Labyrinths – the ones

I would never know how to escape
Without you. Show me your ugly, your
Broken, your devastated,
And force me not to look
Away.

SMOKE AND MIRRORS

Purpose comes easily
In cloistered seclusion
Where conflict is merely
But an illusion.
And, purpose is moot
When clouded by smoke.
Distracted from the point,
We're content to grope

For a new activity
Or the next big thing,
Rather than thinking critically
And using skillful argumentation
As a means of becoming our mirrors' reflection.

ESCAPING THE HEAT

Walking away
From the burn,
Flames lapping
Behind –
A bittersweet
Exit offers motivation,
Yet disbelief,
As new beginnings
Appear through a
Nearby windowpane.
She catches a glimpse
Of the reflection, and
Recognizes herself –
It's been awhile.

RECOLLECTION

I wish I could recall
The firelight
Of late last night
That seemed to summarize it all.

That made
My blackness
Into white, until the whiteness
Was just a lamp-shade,

Luring me back
From a lethargic state,
Asking my sleep to abate
Long enough to turn out the light. So the track

Of a restless mind
Made clear,
Was sadly lost, I fear,
In the sleep I was finally able to find.

REFINEMENT

Fire burning brightly wanes until only
Colored embers light the night

A dusty, crumbling pit
Where once ambition danced

But gradually, a few narrow tapering whips
Lash out, reaching skyward

Exposed to oxygen, a contented balance of
Heat and air are mated,

Fleshing out the
Captivating flames.

SCANDAL

When cheating on a poem with that harlot, Prose –
Whose wordiness rambles
      on and on in those
Elegantly crafted (albeit high-maintenance)
Descriptive rows,
And who seduces with her need for the verbose;
Minding not vanity, nor showing any remorse –
While her acquaintance, Poetry
Strikes a more modest pose,

A schemer is soon inspired
To scrub off the ash (inadvertently gained
By "jumping from the frying pan
Into the fire")
From the scandalous attempt
To give up poetry for Lent.

DUMPING ASH TRAYS IS MESSY BUSINESS

Everyone wants to see
Democratic progress abroad. But
No one likes the mess at home.
Destruction is distressing, for sure –
Devastating for some.
It's depressing.

But progress is always
Borne of pain,
Not sameness.
Change is not conjured up
In some contrived way in a
Smoke-filled room of bygone days.

The dirty ash trays found there
Can't produce clean policies to
Free us from an oppressive past
Become present. Open the windows,
So they won't be broken out.
We need fresh air.

FODDER

I tore your famous
Picture
From a magazine
Today,
To wipe soot from the jar
Of a fancy, red, scented candle I'm currently enjoying, and
you were none the wiser.

But my candle is burning cleanly as a result
Of that slick,
Carbon
Print
Page, sacrificed
For a simple task, assigned.

And that's all we are –
Simple ones,
With simple
Chores;
Fodder,
For the fire that warms another.

OFF AND AWAY

Smoke billowing from
The toaster-oven
Indicates I've
Lost track of
My spirit, again.

It runs off, sometimes,
To fear for the global economy,
Or try and
Make sense
Of me.

"Ding!" the toaster
Rang, but my spirit
Didn't hear it. It
Was busy recalling
Song lyrics.

Now, music
Notes
And
Burnt toast
Smoke

Rise with me.

GENEROSITY

Gave away the shirt on my back,
Then tried to regain composure.
It's hard to do when you're naked.
Plus, the cold turned me bitter.

Thawing was slow, as
Frostbite had set in.
Just when it seemed
I was warming, the shivers worsened

Until new oxygen
Fanned hope
Into a fire. I wait for the blaze
To warm us both.

LEARNING TO INHALE

"To suffocate:
Verb, 1. to kill or choke
By cutting off air..."
Suffocation does not equate
To smothering. not always overdoing,
But sometimes
Under-doing,

Creates imbalance; indeed, a lack of oxygen makes
Breathing difficult.
Exhaling
Day
And night, never inhaling;
Giving and giving,
Never taking,

Never getting, no receiving.
They say living is loving
Then loving
Requires breathing:
Inhale, exhale,
Inhale, exhale,
Inhale...

Chapter II.
Blowing Away

EMBODYING IMAGERY

Don Quixote, your imagination is my muse.
I wish to court her,
As you court your Dulcinea,
To draw insight
From the wind
That turns our mental turbines,

Refusing to be intimidated
By arrogant
Giants who would
Readily defeat us,
Or naïve villagers
Who don't see us

As we truly are.
Your Sancho Panza befriends me – a follower,
Turned leader; Leader, turned follower –
A companion
On this journey of
Endless destinations.

"To draw insight / From the wind/ That turns our mental turbines"
Kingsburn Wind Farm, Stirlingshire.

THANKSGIVING LEFTOVERS

Every Thanksgiving at Mom's request,
Dad drove us around the old homesteads of his past.
Approximately two of the four of us kids would, usually
    begrudgingly, come along.

A windmill here,
An old foundation there,
And every one marked by the same dormant Iowa grasses.

"This is the old French Place,"
He'd say, as he pointed to a partial farmhouse structure.
Or, "Here's the Upper Place." Yes, there was a "Lower Place,"
    too.

Each had-been house
Had its own name, a story.
We'd tease and say, "Where's the old 'new' place?"

Don't it beat all?
I'm becoming more sentimental
Now that he's gone. I'm even using phrases like, "Don't it
    beat all?"

Samantha Terrell   CONFRONTING THE ELEMENTS

When all that's left is advice borrowed from his advice,
And stories about remnants of his old stories,
I'm, finally, grateful Mom made him repeat them every year.

ASHES TO ASHES

The guilt of the generations
Plagues me this morning, settling over me
As a blanket of volcanic ash, and I
Am well rested, but stubbornly
Weary

In my grey-ashen state of angst;
Feeling cold, crass. When confronted by smiles
And everyday things, such joy
Doesn't seem justifiable,
While

There still exists so much hurt. Yet,
I'm surrounded by the carefree,
Who seem to navigate this residual smog
Not only expertly,
But effortlessly,

On auto-
Pilot.
Their smugness swirls around me, a wind,
Stirring up the grit,
Blasting it

Samantha Terrell   CONFRONTING THE ELEMENTS

Into, now irritated,
Eyes
Before re-settling. Until, led from the
Brink of this blinding
Gorge – created by

An erupted cloud of disgust – the
Soiled façade
Becomes clear, establishing –
For good – it's a lush and fertile
Ground that's being fostered.

WE ARE THE WIND

Blowing, gusting –
In winter, snowing;
In summer, dusting.

Where will you take us today?
During this blustery night?
Or at the break of day?

How secretive are your ways –
Where you are going, and
From whence you came.

DEPENDENCIES

Wind is a perspective-giver
In its wafting ways,
Keeping us grounded.
Giving, even as it takes.
Wind is an up-lifter,

As it oppresses,
Pushes, nudges.
It's a priority-keeper.
Who can multi-task amidst a storm gust?
Blowing hard in one's

Dry and tender, wind-burnt face,
It shuts out distractions,
Forcing dependence
Upon its solemn,
Ever-changing grace.

IF ONLY ALL IT TOOK WAS SOAP LEAVES

Little papers, yellowed and rough,
Bound in an over-sized matchbook cover,
Waited to soothe
Mud-caked hands in need of a good wash.
Water trickled from the tap in our old porcelain sink,
Transforming grit

Into smooth,
Dirty into clean,
As paper-thin
Sheets became soap,
And suds became fresh bubbles, capable of evaporating, high
As nature's own leaves would do, on a brisk wind of a serene
    sky.

ILLUSIONS

Allow yourself a moment

In the eating of chicken-salad,
Or a slice of pie.
Allow too, the world its own,
In which to slip silently by,
As tranquil as clouds on wind,
As predictable as guilt on sin.

Find that
Timelessness seems
Not just possible, but apparent.
As though there couldn't otherwise be
Consistency
In nature, ambition, or personality.

Where else
Can we turn
When the faucet has run dry,
Or the candle refuses to burn –
But to the *moment*, which is strikingly different
Than the troublesome *instant*,

Ailing us with its illusion that all is lost.

"Allow too, the world its own/ In which to slip silently by,/ As tranquil as clouds on wind"
Lonely tree, Rannoch Moor.

SCAFFOLDING

You prop me up
On straws of your own making.

I imagine they're steel beams –
Enough to sustain me.

I'm surprised when a gust of wind is
All it takes to knock me down.

But it's a good reminder – your straws
Were never really holding me up.

Plus, scaffolding
Was only ever meant to be temporary.

RESURFACING

After the dust settled
From the wrongdoings,
The weather got windy
And dry. After it blew hard
Day and night, night and day, I tripped
Over the ceaselessly
Sharp tip

Of that hatchet we had buried. After the wound
From my stumble,
I got angry,
Since I never could
Figure why that blade
Had existed
In the first place.

But after I recover
From the recurring hurt,
After I do my
Emotional work,
A callous will form a protective layer over pain,
And with a safe distance,
We'll start again.

"We were specks on aged leaves/ Riding the wind – Riding patterns, of work and parenting"
Lonely tree, Loch Morar.

PASSAGES

The leaves are snowing from the trees
For the third time
Since we've lived here.

The first year, I often sat alone watching,
Taking breaks between unpacking boxes,
Taking calls from your long-distance work.

The second year, we worked together
In the yard – watched together,
As their auburn glory fell, magically, from treetops.

We were specks on aged leaves,
Riding the wind –
Riding patterns, of work and parenting

And habituation of life.
It's widely known rote memorization
Can only carry a person so far.

But, sometimes we need to be carried.
Upon landing, we can afford to feel again, but
We cannot afford to waste any time.

Samantha Terrell   CONFRONTING THE ELEMENTS

We watch more than the leaves this year.
We watch the seasons with reticence.
We watch our lives with caution.

WOODWINDS

To get away,
Play
Night chords –
The ones
Winter welcomes,
And bad dreams

Run from.

Your prize
Is my
Palpitations,
Water and warmth,
Health,
And music

That must come up for air.

WAITING FOR WINTER

It's hard to get clarity in the wind.
Air and emotions swirl.
They keep coming – waves of unresolved feelings
Requiring constant revisiting,
While demanding new processing.

I reach out with futility to grasp the tail-end
Of the last sentiment
But it is already carried away on its kite,
The string having slipped
From my fingers.

I want the wind to be crisp,
Winter chill that nips
Questionable heartaches and honest mistakes
With its biting gusts. But, for now, it's a blustering summer
       one instead – not ideal
For carrying away, once and for all, old uncertainties and
       new anxieties.

WHEN THE SAILS WERE STILL UP

The American experiment
We learned about in school sailed straight
And true, with sails full of the winds of change.

The ocean was large, yet
Our nation was somehow larger.
With Manifest Destiny we claimed her.

But that was only the beginning of the journey.
The real claiming
Was in the taming

Of our hearts,
To deserve her rich peoples
From all the world's corners.

When we were her sailors,
We didn't always steer right, but the sails were,
Indeed, still up. We made corrections to our errors.

Now, sails down,
We watch helplessly
As she blows listlessly,

Samantha Terrell   CONFRONTING THE ELEMENTS

The victim of plutocratic pirates
Fighting over the helm, discussing her direction.
Whichever course is set, presumes to dock her at the same
    sad, destination.

UNTIL THERE'S NOTHING CAN BE DONE

A wind of protest
Whooshes past;
The breeze
Itself a welcome relief,
From the oppressive stench
Of lazy discontent.

But all too quickly, hands
Are bound behind backs,
As the well-oiled
Political machine in its smug glory
Moves on, a carefully built
Conveyor belt

Of deceit,
Attempting to silence those who dare to speak.
Ominously it glides along, evenly paced
Towards the impending cliff edge of space.
Darned if it does seem we're gaining momentum! But in
    which direction?
As we scramble swiftly backward, we're told there's little can
    be done.

BLEAK MIDWINTER

In the bleak midwinter, frosty wind made moan.
Earth stood hard as iron, water like a stone.
-Christina Rosetti

Solemn hawk
In dormant tree
Oversees the warmest,
Yet harshest of winters.

Bold flocks
Refuse to fly in sync,
Stagnating in indecision,
Stalling forward motion –

Except for
The advancement
Of corruption.
Fall-out from

A crumbling core
Summonses
A bleak
Season of anarchy.

PREPARATION

Geese catch a breeze, flying south, and
Apples drop -
Soft spots
Immediately forming,
Small worms burrowing in.

Humankind frets, "Ugh, the weather."
Time
To winterize
Boats, seal
Windows, close deals.

But are we ever really prepared?

"Humankind frets, 'Ugh, the weather."
St Cyrus Beach, Winter.

FIMBULWINTER

An axe age, a sword age
- shields are riven –
a wind age, a wolf age –
before the world goes headlong.
-Seeress's Prophecy

The world went headlong
Into the deep,
Dark spaces
Of climate needs
And plagues
And death,
Disproportionate wealth,

And distrust.
Prevailing
Winds of change
Await
In the fimbulwinter of humanity's new state.
Meanwhile we fumble,
Find footing, stumble

Samantha Terrell   CONFRONTING THE ELEMENTS

Again.
For now, we cloister ourselves
Off in our living rooms,
If we have them, to keep ourselves
Safe from impending doom.
Until we find relief.
Until history repeats.

WHAT IF THERE WERE CLEAN LANDSCAPES?

What if there were clean landscapes?
What if the clutter of humankind
Didn't constantly cloud human minds?

What if there were clean skylines?
What if those clouds, were free to float
Without interference from human things that seem to gloat?

What if we stop being victimized bystanders,
Peering through broken windows at a relentless stream of
    distractions,
Which prevent us from purposeful action?

Live wires strung high
Above the ground may keep us safe,
But smugness always seems to thwart humanity's, "What if?"

UNDERSTANDING

The opposite of right need not be wrong,
As the opposite of silence isn't always a song.
To run is not the only alternative to sitting down;
And, the presence of wind doesn't mean it will be strong.

Consider, anew,
That the sky is more than blue;
And I am okay as me,
And you are okay as you.

"Our arms/ Are fully/ Outstretched tree limbs. Rooted, we pull up
Healthy nutrients of earthbound history."
Looking Towards Schiehallion/ Sìth Chailleann, 'Fairy Hill of the Caledonians.'

Chapter III.
Taking Root

MORNING PEOPLE

Sunrise
Is clouds-rise today –
Overcast, melancholy, grey.
Early fall trees
Are yellow-green
Against the pale sky.

Seasonal changes – foretold
By this palette
Of sad pastels –
Depict the interdependent
Eco-systems
That bring forth new life from old.

Transformations
Of trees
As well as peoples,
Emerge slowly,
From a past tethered by its own gravity,
Contrasted with a future call for revolution.

Samantha Terrell   CONFRONTING THE ELEMENTS

Our arms
Are fully
Outstretched tree limbs. Rooted, we pull up
Healthy nutrients of earthbound history.
Longingly, we draw down Heaven's wisdom and mystery.
Somewhere, behind all the clouds, our sun waits on its
      horizon.

ALLIANCES

It takes a limited number of
Words to convey that our
Earth has always been setting,
Every bit as much as the sun is rising.

But I want more –
Even if many words threatens to
Steal value from the few – because passion
Without meaningful connection

Is devoid of purpose.
So, if we wish to understand the
Simultaneously lengthy and brief, eight
Minutes it takes

For a sunbeam to reach the earth,
We must first pause in respect
For the millions of years it took to form –
Pushing its way from

The center of the sun,
In outward motion,
Striving against forces beyond its control,
In constant pursuit of the fulfillment of its goal.

Samantha Terrell   CONFRONTING THE ELEMENTS

When it finally comes to rest
Upon my arms and shoulders,
I know all of its work, and
All of my words are worth it

Because I've learned of its plight, gained its trust.
And, though the earth may be rising now,
As the sun is setting –
I will forever seek its alliance, never forgetting.

SOUL SUNRISE

Lavender lilac
Petals fall from
The past
On dusty
Dirt roads and
Brittle, dry grass.

The spring wind
That carries the
Scent of the years,
Becomes memory and
Mourning and
Sentimental tears.

Evening dark
Frees the senses to
Rise with the moon.
Night is relief,
Depth, release –
Bringing forth new.

GROWTH

In unfettered fields,
Iris and Poppies bloom
During warm, tender
Days of May and June,
Caterpillars
Begin to creep
Out of cocoons
Where they did sleep,

And, restless souls begin anew, the
Search for that which haunted
While earth
Plodded
Through winter nights –
Roots grew deeper, wings prepared for flight.

ENTRAPMENT

Trapped between
Window and pane,
Moth wings open and shut
Like pages of a book. Dust

Flutters forth
From the cover
Between which words, too,
Are trapped, unable to do

Their work, live and breathe,
Seek and find, call forth action,
Convey the power to believe.
I am a moth. Set me free.

ASCENSION

Descent is never easy.
Sometimes, it's a
Slow-motion sensation.
Though the ground is drawing near, and
That familiar sinking feeling settles in,

It's not welcome. Descent becomes denial.
"Keep looking up!" We tell ourselves and each other.
But all the searching skyward can't deny gravity its pull.
The mind is forced to
Meet the body in a downward lull.

Until,
Earth finally doesn't
Feel so low, again.
And the heart remembers ascension
Was never about rising,
But transformation.

DEBUNKING DESTINY

Fear not for missed opportunity
Or, overshooting destiny.
Surely,

A tree
Does not fear for a
Lack of leaves;

A bird
Does not fear a lack of wings;
The earth does not fear a deficit of dirt.

So, too, day does not fear night,
Nor does death
Fear life.

Let the heart that beats in your chest,
Lead you through your days, and
At night, let your mind lie down and rest.

Destiny is an obstinate creature whose irrelevancy
Is consistently established
By history.

PINE CONE PROPHECIES

Pine cones drip from
Evergreens,
Reaching down in
Anticipation

The way our time machine
Propels us forward –
Predicting where we will go. Then, taking
Us there – a self-fulfilling prophecy.

The pine cone will drop.
We won't be here to see it,
Transported from this place
To another time in space.

A tree/ Does not fear for a/ Lack of leaves;
A bird/ Does not fear a lack of wings;/ The earth does not fear a deficit of dirt.
The Survivor Tree.

LATENCY

The best
The future has to offer
Serenely rests

On a mountain or some valley of our minds
Preparing to
Write stories, cure diseases, solve crimes.

As dew on mountain grasses waits
To evaporate in the morning sun –
Transforms to return to earth as rain –

These, too, shall arise with a transfer of latent energy
Ready to meet
The world's expectancy.

POLARITY

You spoke of oranges and pomegranates, and moonlight on
    the Sea of Galilee
Where your party stood alone – though perhaps,
    accompanied
Amongst hallowed landmarks where great religions were
    forged,
Where our Savior said he brought, not peace, but a sword
And still brings turmoil to the region and all places –
A side-effect of hearts that know both good and evil's faces.
It's a polarity that drives humanity
Both to – and back from – insanity,
Leaving no depths unknown
In the Spirit, or in our earthly home.

FLORA AND FAUNA

Held captive
As
You gaze,
I wonder
How long
This will last.

Your friends, and my own
Rest silently
Nearby
In some lush meadow,
Where, surely,
Soon

I'll join my ancestors
In the earth,
To spring forth
Again; feed your young,
Or dress a table.
When all is lost, loss offers new gains.

WE ARE THE BADLANDS

An absence of foliage
In vast canyons
Gives way to something more,
The opportunity to evoke
Emotion from its expanse.
Variegated cutaways of
Ancient earth
Rise and fall
The same way my body
Shudders at your embrace.
What great equalizer
Cuts through earth and
Our bodies, but Time?
And we are all, merely,
Nature laid bare,
Shrouded only
By the eyes of God.

"Variegated cutaways of/ Ancient earth/ Rise and fall"
The Quirang, Skye.

"... a wind age, a wolf age – before the world goes headlong."
Callanish Stones on the Isle of Lewis.

NEOLITHIC ERA

Did the Neolithic
Gaze upon the dandelions?
Or, did they graze upon them instead?
And, what was the significance of their stones?

We tread upon dandelions,
And cover the earth in concrete,
Whilst searching the past for answers
To questions the present readily provides.

If only we would gaze upon the fields,
Bask in the sun,
Call our current existence to the task
Of plodding, yes, but lightly.

PROMISCUITY

Obnoxious peoples,
Gaudy and loud,
And their neon signs – pink, yellow, red –

Drown out
The tranquil
Green of nature.

A flashy, self-promoting crowd
In steel towers,
Steal flowers.

Its inhabitants
Endorse their greed
While earth waits quietly under concrete.

SEEKING THE PROMISED RAINBOW

Red and golden trees
Against a greying
Early-winter sky,
Comfort me
While I mourn
Your losses
As if they were my own.

I've overdue concern for
Future ones
Whose lives are mere saplings – when
The world
We've created in haste
To protect ourselves – and them, allegedly – is
Filled with empty artillery shells and nuclear waste.

The earth cries
Down its rain, and
Some of us cry with it,
Reaching, with the trees, towards the sky,
To wonder on solutions
That will salvage order in our sorrowful hearts,
And this suffering creation.

ESCAPING ARROGANCE

From the rocky cliff side
Where we tremble, I see
Gulls, below, freely
Feeding on puddles and pride
While we dream of deliverance from this craggy place.

A man who comes
Down the mountain to meet us,
Has found his happiness.
He delivers it with a kiss.
And then, he's off! Easily slicing through rising waters,

As a butcher knife through butter.
He's carefree,
Not worried
About the puddles,
Let alone his pride.

Inspired, I try
To gather in
The children
And the vulnerable, forgetting I,
Too, am one who feels.

But the birds have seen it all. They sometimes cry
For us –
Stuck
As we are – afraid of falling, unable to fly.
The only option left, is to climb.

WRITING MY EPITAPH

My ghosts already haunt me –
Ghosts of poor choices and things
I shouldn't have said;
Ghosts which sneak up around my grave,
Exposing deeply-buried,
Long-loathed parts of me
That haven't fully decayed.

The rotting,
Fleshy bits
Hanging in
Their grotesque way, remind me they wait,
Encourage me to address
Their morbid presence,
Pick them apart, and bury them again so they may properly
    deteriorate.

Samantha Terrell   CONFRONTING THE ELEMENTS

My ghosts long
For fertile earth,
For healthy new growth.
When they come haunting, they make a compelling case.
They are translucent, persistent beings, not unlike the
    memories
They dredge up to share with me.
Sometimes, they nearly convince me I'm dead. But why is
    my headstone blank?

Despite their evil intent as
They accompany me through vast graveyards,
I must, instead, see orchards
Of opportunity. Abashed,
But not yet defeated, I'll seek
A harvest of good deeds
For my future epitaph.

"Reminding me they wait for me/ To address their presence, pick them apart and Bury them again"
Culloden Moor, the Graves of the Clans.

ON GRAVITY

Time fell forward, once
Again, while I wasn't
Watching.
Even its weighty
Hour-hand succumbed
To gravity's pull.
I was busy, waiting – at bus stops, in washrooms,
On airplanes, and classrooms;

In offices and boardrooms,
Park playgrounds and nursery rooms –
With sleep-deprived eyes, shielded
From the repeated
Accosting
Of the pull towards morning.

GROUNDED

Backing slowly
Out of Plato's cave,
The promise of an orange
Sunset awaits.

Armed only
With the blueprints
Of perspective, unsure of the foothold
To be found, but confident

The sole
Will meet earth's floor,
Confident the world
Will be met with the soul's core.

The sole/ Will meet earth's floor,
Elgol, Sunset, Skye.

ACKNOWLEDGMENTS

The concept for *Confronting the Elements* came into being after having my chapbook *Keeping Afloat* published by JC STUDIO Press in 2021. Since *Keeping Afloat* features water-inspired poetry, it only seemed right to give the other elements a showcase of their own. After constructing the manuscript, I happened into an amazing opportunity to have this book published simultaneously by two of the most generous and supportive indie presses I've encountered. Thus, my heartfelt thanks goes to Revolutionary Press, who gave my work a home as a serialization in *Revolutionary Review*; and, to Jane Cornwell of JC STUDIO Press, for the illustrations and the publish of this book in its final form. Last but not least, I'd like to extend my thanks to these fine publications, media outlets, and/or websites where the following individual poems previously appeared or aired:

Thanksgiving Leftovers – *Dwelling Literary*

Embodying Imagery; Off and Away – *Fevers of the Mind*

Coaxing Out Existence – audio file aired by
Eat the Storms Podcast (Dublin, Ireland); and
Express Yourself Sunny G Radio (Glasgow, Scotland)

Morning People; Alliances – *In Parentheses*

Polarity – *LogoSophia Magazine*

Dumping Ash Trays Is Messy Business – *Nine Cloud Journal*

Woodwinds – *Paddler Press*

Ascension; Autumn Winds; Entrapment; Flora and Fauna; Latency; Neolithic Era; Objects of Reflection; We Are the Badlands; When the Sails Were Still Up; Writing My Epitaph – *The Wombwell Rainbow*

About Samantha Terrell

Samantha Terrell is an internationally published poet and author of multiple five-star collections. Her poetry, which emphasizes self-awareness as a means to social awareness, can be found in a variety of publications including: *Dissident Voice, Dove Tales, Green Ink Poetry, In Parentheses, Misfit Magazine, Nine Cloud Journal, Paddler Press, Poetry Quarterly, Red Weather,* and many others. Terrell is a wife, mother, and former manager in the nonprofit sector. She writes from her home in upstate New York.

Find her online at: www.SamanthaTerrell.com.

Other Books by Samantha Terrell

Vision, and Other Things We Hide From
(Potter's Grove Press, 2021)

Keeping Afloat
(JC STUDIO Press, 2021)

Simplicity, and Other Things We Overcomplicate
(2022)

Things Worth Repeating?
(2022)

A Self-Taught Poet's Handbook for Self-Taught Poets
(2022)

Cosmic Tragicomedy
(2022)

Artwork

1. Buachaille Etive Mòr
2. The Muir Burn
3. Peat Burning
4. The Lost Valley, or Coire Gabhail, Glencoe
5. Ineous, Grangemouth
6. Kingsburn Wind Farm, Stirlingshire
7. The Lonely Tree, Rannoch Moor
8. The Lonely Tree, Loch Morar
9. St Cyrus Beach, Winter
10. Looking Towards Schiehallion
11. The Survivor Tree, Carrifran Valley
12. The Quirang, Skye
13. Callanish Stones on the Isle of Lewis
14. Culloden Moor, the Graves of the Clans
15. Elgol, Stormy Sunset, Skye

I jumped at the chance to put another poetry collection together with Samantha Terrell, aka Honesty Poetry. This was a perfect opportunity to produce some 'honest' artwork. So these are 'old school' watercolours, mostly produced during little road trips around Scotland, in an A4 sketchpad, usually working from life, with my paints balanced on my knees and waterpot on the dashboard, very often torrential rain battering the windscreen, car buffeted by the gales. Almost confronting the elements.

I've been reading a lot about the use of AI in art and how it is being used to replace human artists. To me, this seems souless and pointless.

These little paintings were done for pure pleasure in response to Samantha's words. A joy project. I hope you enjoy our book as much as I've enjoyed putting it together.

About Jane Cornwell

Jane is an artist, illustrator and designer. After responding to a call out for an artist to provide 30 prompt art works for a National Poetry Month Ekphrastic Challenge, 2020, by Paul Brookes on Twitter, she discovered that she really enjoys poetry. Since then, she's collaborated with Paul Brookes, Samantha Terrell and Susan Richardson to create poetry books, with some more to follow from her very small press, Jane's Studio Press.

Jane has exhibited with the RSW at the National Gallery of Scotland, The Big Art Show, Glasgow, SSA, Knock Castle Gallery, Aberdeen Artists Society, The Glasgow Group, Paisley Art Institute, MacMillan Exhibition at Bonhams, Edinburgh, The House For An Art Lover, Pittenweem Arts Festival, Compass Gallery, The Revive Show, East Linton Art Exhibition and Strathkelvin Annual Art Exhibition.

Jane is a member of Publishing Scotland, the Association of Illustrators and the Society of Childrens Book Writers and Illustrators - British Isles. She graduated with a BA(hons) Design from Glasgow School of Art, age 20.

Her website is: www.janecornwell.co.uk.

Made in the USA
Middletown, DE
02 August 2023